This is Home

Poetry Collection

Loni Hoots

Author Note

Dear Reader,

This short poetry collection dives into the complexity of growing up in a household where each family member dives into the uniqueness of growing up and growing apart from one another. Lingering emotions, unfinished conversations, the feeling of being unwanted or not feeling like an integral part of the family- these poems dive into that while tackling the complex moments of trying to make things work and fix the cracks within the family foundation. It is in the form of a dollhouse that these poems take place, as if each poem is a member of the family put on full display as if it were an actor a child uses for their own stories.

Enjoy the collection!

Loni Hoots

Contents

Author Note 4

Diner Booth 7

One Winter Day 8

Coming Home 9

Open Books 10

Strangers 11

Glasses 12

Fell for the Idea 13

The Box Under the Porch 14

Sycamore Trees 16

Being Human 17

Sanctuary 18

About to Appear 19

Ghost of You 20

The Weatherman 21

The Rain 22

A Hundred Lives 23

Letter for Bella 24

The Richest Man 25

Powerless 26

Saying Goodbye 28

Lights Off 29

Into the Void 30

A Heavy Heart 31

Peepoonki 32

Patiently Waiting 33

Daggers 34

Message in our Dreams 35

The Long Run 36
Wrong Direction 37
Will I ever Stop Running? 38
Lingering Past 39
Bedroom Kid 40
If I Listened 41
Always Searching 42
Tunnel 43
Lost Together 44
Time will Tell 45
Chess Pieces 46
Alive 47
When You Did 48
Car Ride 49

Diner Booth

One booth,
two cups,
one filled with coffee
the other with tea,
absolutely nothing chaotic,
everything is playing out peacefully.

The snow turns the city
into a winter wonderland right outside the doors,
as you and I build a bond
that's as strong as this diner's foundation,
sturdy and determined,
reliable yet gentle,
a bond that I had only dreamt of years before.

One Winter Day

A gentle caress that seems
to place cement between the scars,
not only on my face and arms,
but in my heart and soul,
where it had been ripped and torn apart.

As snow continues to swirl about
one thing is certain,
you are the one my soul has been searching for,
this lets me know that the search is over,
it all happened on this winter day,
while I was out and about.

Coming Home

Come now, gentle soul,
the snow is waiting
as I urge you to make your way home,
before the sun sets under the trees,
before every limb
succumbs to the cruel breeze.

A light is turned on,
waiting for you to make it to the steps,
hoping you don't fumble down the frozen path.

Hopefully, you're bundled up,
with woolen mittens on your hands,
while your tender heart
is protected with a thick woolen jacket.

Open Books

Books everywhere,
in shelves,
on the floor,
spilling out of the backpack.
There's never enough,
yet, there's only little space
to put them.
Each one opened to a different page,
waiting for me to return once again.
Sighs escape each book,
just like the sounds that escape my mouth.
I whisper to the books
"I'll return tonight,
once every soul in the house
has fallen asleep."
For they don't need to
know where I run off to
when I should be sleeping.

Strangers

It's so strange
that others will take a look in,
see only blood,
but do not know the story within.
Each of us has a room,
but not a soul lingers too long,
like strangers in the night
we're floating along.
A mother,
a father,
children too,
one might think they'd belong,
but something about this
doesn't quite fit,
as if the characters aren't meant
for this household,
yet, they need to stay here
till their own stories begin.

Glasses

Not once have I looked
with rose colored glasses,
for those won't do.
The glasses that were chosen
harness a unique ability,
one where others deem it to be dark,
but I know its true capabilities.

Ancient text mixed with Gothic fairytales
induce scenes that no one else dreams.
True love's kiss set in a sleepy hollow
speaks as if it were in complete harmony.
Whispering melodies along the riverbank
as nature whistles back
garnering the attention of those it desires.

No.
No rose-colored glasses needed,
for these stained colored glasses fit perfectly,
and only a few are given.

Fell for the Idea

Lying awake in the morning
golden hour seeps across the room
as I'm thinking out loud
wondering why I can't speak your name,
it's as if I only fell for the idea of you,
so, all I can do is to let it all fade,
along with the clouds that never wanted to stay.

My chest tightens every time you are around,
making it harder to breathe,
forcing me to shut down
cause I can't get over the what ifs,
or I'll just look like a clown,
which is the last thing I want.

It sucks to even speak sometimes
cause it feels like I'm about to blast off,
throw up this realization
that I fell for the idea of you,
an image contorted to fit this version
that sits in my head,
now, it's time to sing to the golden hour of night,
and see you tomorrow.

The Box Under the Porch

It has been over a decade since we stepped foot inside the house
we grew up,
in fact, it has been over a decade since we buried our hopes and
dreams,
the future we hoped everything would be
into a tiny box.

If we were to go back to our childhood home,
would the box still be buried there?
Would we find the lives we wanted so much
frozen in time?
There are so many questions,
and so many things we constantly wonder about,
yet, we will never know if those dreams will come to life
till we witness them come true.

A life all our own,
one where the universe and God would guide us to,
one where I would educate the minds of little ones,
live a life where all your wildest dreams would come true,
as the world around us moved in sync,
granting all the hopes and dreams to those who believed.

Now the question is,
are we living the lives we dreamt we would have?
The ones that pushed us down the correct paths?
If not, then that is okay,
cause we still have an entire lifetime
to pursue the dreams,

we left in the box under the porch twenty years ago.
Always searching,
Always searching for a space somewhere I can close my eyes
and get away,
I still try to cover my tracks,
yet it's never enough,
cause I still get found
even though I don't want to be.
Always searching for my place,
but I'm running out of spaces that I can call mine,
I'm getting tired,
and need to find somewhere
I can lay my head
even if it's for the night.
Tired of constant detours,
always told to turn right
when it leads me to a dead end,
my conclusions have led me to believe
that I've been listening to the wrong ones,
they led me on endless searches,
I still feel
that I'm going to keep on searching,
but it's going to lead me
to where I'm supposed to be.

Sycamore Trees

Sycamore trees whisper as I lay underneath,
so, all I can do is lie quietly.
Mother once told me stories
of a love so sweet,
yet, all they seem is bittersweet dreams.
It feels as if it wishes to repeat,
being the one to grant it or not,
I send it on the waves of the wind,
making sure it doesn't come back like a slingshot.
Laying my head on the grass,
the Sycamore trees whisper sweetly,
granting only serenity,
as the old wishes disappear,
making way for new ones to appear.

Being Human

Exhaustion runs through my body,
attempting to tear me to pieces,
but there's something that it doesn't know,
 it doesn't know what I'm capable of,
nor is it prepared for what's to come,
and I can't wait to see the look on its face.
Forged in a vase that was molded by fire,
designed by the faces of my ancestors,
baptized by the tears of my foremothers,
my emotions are vast, just like my ambitions.
I feel lost most of the time,
there's a part of me
that can't help but wonder,
wonder if what I'm doing is right,
or if there's another path that is ready for me.
Is being human all about being lost?
How do we find ourselves?
Exhaustion is taking its toll,
and I'm barely hanging on,
cause these rocky roads are causing me to slip,
and I don't know
if I'll be able to get a good grip.

Sanctuary

Deep in the pit of my soul
a rush of new life is seeping in,
as if everything before never existed,
as though every thought and dream
are finally receiving its blessing.
Calmness rushes down my face,
letting my soul return
while I allow myself to take the first step
inside this new place.
Winter flows dreamily down the river,
as Spring makes her appearance,
it no longer hurts
to walk amongst the others,
for I am on a journey
to a place hidden by the naked eye,
I walk in peace,
I walk in strength,
I am walking to the sanctuary
that calls me in the dead of the night.

About to Appear

It's no longer serving me
and it feels like my skin is on fire
as I lay here on the floor
letting me perspire.
The night is drifting away
the morning is almost here
it feels funny to say
that I know something is about to appear.
Who is knocking at the door?
What is this feeling in my chest?
So many questions
but I don't want to be a bore,
instead, I'll lay here
and wait for the downpour
cause I'm shattering now, my brain has left
but I'm no longer asking what to do,
cause something is about to appear.

Ghost of You

I could swallow these pills,
watch as the ghost of you slips away,
I could drown the sound
but what good would that do?
When all I wanted was
someone to talk to,
and not be jealous
of the ghost of you.
Branded by fire
I refuse to give you another chance.
You can say what you want
it will only fall into the void,
as I move forward without a second glance.

The Weatherman

It's raining outside,
walls are closing in,
here I am watching the weatherman,
hoping some light will break through,
let me out before I go mad.
Streets empty,
cars all at home,
ignoring the signs
cause I want to feel other than alone.
No need to change the channel,
it's nonsense anyways,
watching the weatherman helps,
cause it keeps the noise away.
11 pm, and it's still the same,
just another routine stop
where the channel stays fixed on the weatherman
as I down another edible to drown out the pain.

The Rain

Just like the rain
you came out of nowhere and hid behind clouds,
letting all the pain
come crashing down.
Swirls of ecstasy
lingered in the air,
while the past began decaying,
and you not giving a care.
Here you are,
better than before,
stronger than the rain,
the name you once bore.

A Hundred Lives

I've pictured a hundred lives,
ones where I'd wake up in a different bed
and a different life,
not a soul in the family ever noticed
that I wasn't there.
Tried to make sense of it,
tried to shake the thoughts out of my head,
but it kept happening.
My back against the wall
as my mind continued,
running from one life to another.
I've pictured a hundred lives,
ones where I'm happy,
far away from the sadness
that fills my drowning heart.
Yet, no one notices,
and I keep running from one life
to the next.

Letter to Bella

Can you tell me
what it looks like?
Is it filled with green pastures and an endless sky?
Are you feeling better
knowing there are no more thunderstorms
that used to make you hide?
And do you run around
like you did when you were by my side?
Sometimes, it feels lonely
without you by my side,
but deep in my heart, this is better,
cause you get to sleep soundly in the greenest hillsides.

The Richest Man

Many believe that riches
only come in the form of money,
but that's not the case.
For it is the man whose children run to
when his arms are empty,
when he's had a long day.
He sacrifices everything,
refuses to complain,
knowing his hard work is more than appreciated.
He knows he is praised,
loved, noticed,
and the most valuable figure.
Not for a minute does he question
the riches he's been blessed with,
for everything he could ever ask for
comes from his children
whom he adores.

Powerless

I've paid my dues,
then some more,
now I've got something to say,
but there's a lot on my mind
and it's getting in the way.
I try and try,
every single day, I try
yet, I still can't find the right way
to say it, and it's leaving me sleepless.
What am I doing?
Why can't I open my mouth?
It shouldn't be this hard,
yet here I am,
lying in bed
listening to the thunder rage outside my window.
You know what?
No.
I'm not doing this anymore,
I can't stand the silence another second,
prepare yourselves,
cause I'm taking my voice back and
 silencing those who dare make me feel powerless.
I'm not a little girl anymore,
I don't hide in dark corners
or bow to those who think they're superior,
cause I'm not powerless,
I'm powerful, and I'm here to embrace it.
Slow down
pace yourself,

lest you stumble and fall,
for life's crossroads await,
and the choices won't be gentle.
Yield to the universe's gentle hand,
unwind the knots of time,
and softly glide through life's tender dance,
by living and loving your life.

Saying Goodbye

Let your soul rest,
let your shadow lay down.
Let your heart ache,
wait till the sun rises,
then join me in putting this to bed.

Lights Off

Oh, darling girl,
how did you get up there?
How did you get up so high?
Are you trying to flee?
Run into the night?

There have been times it's like that,
you want to breathe,
so, you escape,
as quickly as you can,
as quickly as the lights turn off.
The world tries to hold you down,
but even you know
you're not meant to stay grounded,
so,
you take off into the night,
once the lights turn off.

Into the Void

The world continues on
as my mind succumbs to the silence,
everyone around me chats
while my soul jumps into the void,
along with my conscience.

No one knows,
not an inkling,
as though I were never part
of this world,
and only meant to jump from one line to the next.
Who knows where I'm about to go,
but all I know is this,
I am slowly vanishing into the wind,
but I'm ready to take flight,
and waiting to see where I land.

A Heavy Heart

Please be patient with me,
I'm healing,
and my heart is still a little heavy,
so, hold my hand
and walk side by side,
as I patch up the wounds
that were left to weaken.

Peepoonki

As we watch the frost
make its way across the pond
and morning dew,
our soul comes alive
as we hunker
for hibernation
and brace for the harsh changes
as Mother Earth heals,
just like we do.

*Peepoonki is my from my tribal language, Miami. It means "It Is Winter."

Patiently Waiting

Empty halls are all that's left,
as I sleep on the floor
with nothing but a pillow and blanket,
with the rest of my things
packed into three suitcases.

No one.
not a single soul knows,
by dawn, I'll be gone,
leaving a vacant home
overlooking the city
I thought I'd call my own.

For too long
I've ran,
but that never mattered,
it was bound to happen.
My true self would swim up,
grab a hold
and drag me back to the ocean floor
where everyone was patiently waiting,
knowing I'd soon return,
after trying so hard not to be me.

Daggers

Your words are like daggers,
each word cuts deeper
than the last
so, I urge you to leave me be
if you don't dare to be
my peace.

Message in our Dreams

From time to time
I visit again,
it's always in my dreams,
it still feels the same,
nothing has changed,
at least what I can tell,
yet, there's always something new
that is trying to tell me
what my heart and mind fight
to tell me in my waking life.

What is it?
What are they trying to tell me?
Is there something I missed?
Reality never lets us know what's right or wrong,
it allows us to make decisions,
till it is time to lay our head
on the pillow at night,
wait for the message that we need,
yet, they are constantly scrambled
leaving us confused when we wake.

The Long Run

Found myself wondering
about the door I just opened,
I no longer worry about what lies ahead,
cause everything is now showing
itself to me in a new way,
in the form of glimpses
of scenes that are to come soon.

People around me tell me they worry,
but I know that I'm not scared,
and look at them with a knowing look,
telling them, "I'll see you in the long run,"
before I take off.

Wrong Direction

Some say life can steal your eyes
attempting to steer you in the wrong direction,
not caring what may come next,
but I'm here to tell you,
that they don't know what's best for you,
just because they have these rules,
it doesn't mean it's meant for you.

We're often mistaken
about what is meant for us,
or who we're supposed to hold onto,
cause life thinks it can
dictate what's best,
yet, it doesn't realize that
we're not meant for any wrong directions,
unlike the rest of them.

Will I ever Stop Running?

All I've ever done is run,
run from my past,
run from my myself,
run as far as I could and fast as I could.
There were times when I jogged,
thinking that would help,
but it kept creeping up,
like the hounds escaping hell.

I'm tired,
I just want to rest,
When will I stop running?
cause I'm exhausted,
and want to feel safe,
not constantly battling.

Lingering Past

Windows rolled down,
wind ripping through my hair,
as ambient music courses through my veins,
as I attempt to not look in the mirror.

No other car for the past several miles,
yet, I can still see my past
lingering in the rearview mirror,
as if it were being dragged
by a rope attached to the back of the car.
If I push the gas pedal,
it creeps back up,
if I stop,
it stops and watches to see what I'll do,
will I ever get away from my past?
Highly doubt it,
maybe I need to pull over,
get out,
and walk up to it,
giving it the greenlight
to detach and wish me luck.

Bedroom Kid

The world isn't meant for kids like me,
the ones who are afraid to even step on the porch,
and be seen with the family.
It's not from embarrassment,
but of fear,
of not being sure if
anyone will accept us,
and just stare.
The world hasn't always been kind,
and we can see right through,
so, instead of handling it like everyone else,
we just shut ourselves in our rooms.

If I Listened

I'm feeling a little mixed up,
cause all I hear are inaudible voices,
none of them are what I want to hear,
and it's becoming clear,
but it's burning me up
just thinking about it,
as if I'm fighting what my soul wants.

It hurts a little more every day,
but it wouldn't if I listened,
cause when I hurt,
you hurt too,
just like I do
when you are fighting the emotions in the same ring.
When are we going to accept it?
When we were knocked out?
And our ears are filled with ringing?

If I listened
I wouldn't be here,
all I can do is just believe,
that by the morning
everything will be okay,
and I'll move on with you.

Always Searching

Always searching for a space
somewhere, I can close my eyes,
and get away,
I still try to cover my tracks,
yet, it's never enough,
cause I still get found,
even though I don't want to be.

Always searching for my place
but I'm running out of spaces
that I can call mine,
I'm getting tired,
and need to find somewhere I can lay my head,
even if it is for the night.

Tired of constant detours,
always told to turn right,
when it leads me to a dead,
my conclusions have led me to believe,
that I've been listening to the wrong ones,
they led me on endless searches,
I still feel that I'm going to keep on searching,
but it's going to lead me,
to where I'm supposed to be.

Tunnel

I don't want to live here anymore,
the morning has risen once again,
yet, it hasn't changed anything in this house.
Positivity is a rarity in this place,
all that is heard are yells and curses,
can't tell if we are friends or enemies,
it's hard to tell in the darkness of this tunnel,
because neither one of us
is willing to work towards the light at the end.
One of us has to be willing to walk,
yet we're both too stubborn,
so, we just sit there
and stare,
figuring out what to do next.

Lost Together

It's like you say all the time,
"We're lost together in this world,"
I look at you like you've lost your mind,
just like you do when I've lost mine.
There's something always needing work,
I heard that's what it's like,
relationships don't bloom overnight,
it takes time.

Time is barely heard,
when two souls attempt
to muster through the world,
with little eyes on them,
watching every moment,
seeing how they handle
everything that is thrown their way.

Time will Tell

Fumbling around in the dark,
ghosts of the past try to hold me down,
I call out your name,
praying you will be there,
just like you said you'd be.
Till you get here,
I'll keep my eyes on the tracks,
cause only time will tell,
when you will appear,
that's how the old story goes.

Chess Pieces

The past can come back
in ways you never expected,
the melody of a tune
reminds you of someone you forgot,
or a scent takes you back to when
you were truly innocent.

Time moves on,
people come and go,
new memories are made,
yet, somehow, the past makes its way back,
but in the most unusual way.

This time it's not so scary,
instead, you look at it,
with fresh new eyes
and realize that something was hidden,
like an easter egg,
with the best prize.
That small piece of the past creeps in,
you're okay with it,
cause it shapes you
into the version of who you need to be
to move to the next space,
cause soon,
you'll be screaming, "Checkmate!"

Alive

I know people talk,
I don't care,
let them,
so, we can continue to walk,
what they say doesn't matter,
cause everything tends to blur,
just like the city lights
when the train rips through.

The colors of the night
reflect in your eyes,
it's easy to see your soul,
it lights up every time you feel alive,
and I want to feel that too,
I'm ready to take your hand,
and be consumed.

When You Did

Between you and I
I've lost my mind,
couldn't tell when it happened,
but I'm leaving it behind.

Records play to an empty apartment,
It's easier said than done,
when everyone says,
"Pick up and move on."

The world is lost, and so am I,
where has my heart gone,
it feels like I'm trapped.
The night birds sing,
drowning out the TV,
I'm on the floor,
glad you found me when you did,
cause who knows what
winter may have done.

Car Ride

We could leave for a few hours,
take the car,
drive through the countryside,
letting the wind fill the car,
as the music escapes to the landscape.
Let's go somewhere,
this house is not where we need to be,
it's filled with sadness,
it's filled with resentment,
we need to be elsewhere,
anywhere that allows the old energy to leave.